Crowned Image Publishing

Copyright © 2017

Printed in the United States of America.

ISBN-13: 978-1-946622-02-0

KNOWING GOD KNOWING OTHERS

NEW SONG NASHVILLE
25TH
EST 1993
Anniversary
TWENTY FIVE YEARS

_____

name

_____

date started

_____

date completed

REACHING
NEIGHBORS, NATIONS AND GENERATIONS
WITH THE GOOD NEWS
OF JESUS CHRIST'S
LOVE AND POWER

VISION STATEMENT

Reach UP To God
Through the ministries of prayer and praise.

Reach IN To One Another
Through the ministries of making disciples, multiplying covenantal community and developing leaders.

Reach OUT To The World
Through the ministries of evangelism, compassion and justice.

MINISTRY VALUES

- The Ministries of Prayer & Praise
  (Matthew 6:6, Psalm 145:2)

- The Ministries of Evangelism & Making Disciples
  (Mark 16:15-16, Matthew 28:18-20)

- The Ministries of Developing Leaders
  (2 Timothy 2:2)

- The Ministries of Multiplying Covenantal Community
  (Hebrews 10:24-25)

- The Ministries of Compassion and Justice
  (Zechariah 7:9)

REACH UP TO GOD
through the ministries
of prayer and praise.

REACH UP
PRAYER & PRAISE

As you engage daily in the ministries of prayer and praise, use the following scriptures to guide you. Use the spaces on the following pages to list both your requests to the Lord and when He answered.

PRAYER : But you, when you pray, go into your room, and when you have shut your door, pray to your Father who is in the secret place, and your Father who sees in secret will reward you openly (Matthew 6:6).

PRAISE : Every day I will bless You, And I will praise Your name forever and ever (Psalm 145:2).

PRAYING THE WAY JESUS TAUGHT

In this manner, therefore, pray: Our Father in heaven, hallowed be Your name. Your kingdom come. Your will be done on earth as it is in heaven. Give us this day our daily bread. And forgive us our debts, as we forgive our debtors. And do not lead us into temptation, but deliver us from the evil one. For Yours is the kingdom and the power and the glory forever. Amen (Matthew 6:9-13).

"OUR FATHER IN HEAVEN":
Affirm your identity as a child of God.

"HALLOWED BE YOUR NAME":
Hallowed means held in awe, revered. Praise and thank God for who He is, what He has done, and what He will do. As the Holy Spirit leads, include in your prayer the names of God:

THE NAMES OF GOD:
- **El Elyon** | "God Most High" (Gen.14:18)
- **El Roi** | "God Who Sees" (Gen.16:13)
- **El Shaddai** | "God Almighty" (Gen.17:1)
- **Yahweh Jireh** | "The Lord Will Provide" (Gen.22:14)
- **Yahweh Rophe** | "The Lord Who Heals" (Exo.15:26)
- **Yahweh Nissi** | "The Lord My Banner" (Exo.17:15)
- **Yahweh M'Kaddesh** | "The Lord Who Sanctifies You" (Exo.31:13)
- **Yahweh Shalom** | "The Lord Is Peace" (Jdg.6:24)
- **Yahweh Rohi** | "The Lord My Shepherd" (Psa.23:1)

- **Yahweh Tsidkenu** | "The Lord Our Righteousness" (Jer.23:6)

- **Yahweh Sabaoth** | "The Lord of Hosts" (1 Sam.1:3)

- **Yahweh Shammah** | "The Lord Is There" (Eze.48:35)

"YOUR KINGDOM COME. YOUR WILL BE DONE ON EARTH AS IT IS IN HEAVEN":

Pray for God's purposes and plans:
Globally | Nationally | Locally | Congregationally | Personally

"GIVE US THIS DAY OUR DAILY BREAD":

You never know how much God will get to you if He knows He can get it through you (to others). God promises to meet our needs, but we are to show our dependency on Him and ask for what we need to receive from Him for others. Pray dependently, consistently, specifically, and expectantly for your and others' physical, emotional and spiritual needs.

"FORGIVE US OUR DEBTS, AS WE FORGIVE OUR DEBTORS":

Ask the Holy Spirit to show you where you need to:
- Receive God's forgiveness for your sins through confession, repentance and cleansing (1 John 1:9).

- Release God's forgiveness to others who have sinned against you, and cancel their debt (Mark 11:25-26).

"DO NOT LEAD US (ALLOW US TO BE LED) INTO TEMPTATION, BUT DELIVER US FROM THE EVIL ONE:

Take particular areas of temptation before the Lord, surrendering

to God's strength and protection. Take authority over the enemy, committing both to resist his attacks and not to go where you shouldn't be, as there is no grace to resist temptation in those circumstances.

"YOURS IS THE KINGDOM AND THE POWER AND THE GLORY FOREVER":

- The Kingdom: Rest in the knowledge that God's rule and dominion is working in and around us.

- The Power: Rely on God's dynamic, abundant, mighty, miracle-working, and creative power, knowing that we stand and fight from a place of victory.

- The Glory: Reflect God's excellence, honor, beauty, majesty and splendor to the world!

SCRIPTURES FOR
COMMON PRAYER NEEDS

When we pray Scripture, we say that we agree with the truth of God's Word. Just as an anchor keeps a ship from being tossed to and fro, the Word of God is an anchor for our prayers that gives us a guide so that we are not moved off course. Also, when we use His Word in prayer, we walk in the authority and power of His truth.

In this section, many common prayer points have been outlined to help you as you grow in prayer. For example, if one of your friends is sick, you can look through the Scriptures under the "Healing" section and pray for your friend. Your prayer may look like this: Lord Jesus, thank You that You were beaten so that we could be whole. Your wounds have healed us, and so I ask that You would heal my friend. In the name of Jesus I pray, Amen.

(All scripture quotations listed in this section are taken from The New International Reader's Version®, NIRV®, Copyright © 1995, 1996, 1998, 2014 by Biblica, Inc.®. Used by permission. All rights reserved worldwide.)

RELATIONSHIP WITH GOD

+ I will ask the Father. And He will give you another Friend to help you and to be with you forever. The Friend is the Spirit of truth. The world can't accept Him. That is because the world does not see Him or know Him. But you know Him. He lives with you, and He will be in you (John 14:16-17).

+ Jesus replied, "Anyone who loves Me will obey My teaching. My Father will love him. We will come to him and make Our home with him" (John 14:23).

+ Jesus replied, "Love the Lord your God with all your heart and with all your soul. Love Him with all your mind" (Matthew 22:37).

+ God loved the world so much that He gave His one and only Son. Anyone who believes in Him will not die but will have eternal life (John 3:16).

+ I am absolutely sure that not even death or life can separate us from God's love. Not even angels or demons, the present or the future, or any powers can do that. Not even the highest places or the lowest, or anthing else in all creation can do that. Nothing at all can ever separate us from God's love because of what Christ Jesus our Lord has done (Romans 8:38-39).

PEACE

+ Blessed are those who make peace. They will be called sons of God (Matthew 5:9).

+ May glory be given to God in the highest heaven! And may peace be given to those He is pleased with on earth (Luke 2:14)!

HEALING

+ Jesus was beaten so we could be whole. His wounds have healed us (Isaiah 53:5).

+ Jesus personally carried away our sins in His own body on the cross so we can be dead to sin and live for what is right. You have been healed by His wounds (1 Peter 2:24)!

+ …You will be able to destroy all the power of the enemy. Nothing will harm you (Luke 10:19).

+ What I'm about to tell you is true. What you lock on earth will be locked in heaven. What you unlock on earth will be unlocked in heaven. Again, here is what I tell you. Suppose two of you on earth agree about anything you ask for. My Father in heaven will do it for you (Matthew 18:18-19).

+ He said, If you listen carefully to the voice of the LORD your God and do what is right in His eyes, if you pay attention to His commands and keep all His decrees, I will not bring on you any of the diseases I brought on the Egyptians, for I am the Lord, who heals you (Exodus 15:26).

+ And my God will meet all your needs according to His glorious riches in Christ Jesus (Philippians 4:19).

UNBELIEVERS

+ God said, "Let light shine out of darkness" (Genesis 1:3).

+ He made His light shine in our hearts. It shows us the light of God's glory in the face of Christ (2 Corinthians 4:6).

+ In the same way, let your light shine in front of others. Then they will see the good things you do. And they will praise your Father who is in heaven (Matthew 5:16).

+ When He comes, He will prove that the world's people are guilty. He will prove their guilt concerning sin and godliness and judgment (John 16:8).

+ God loved the world so much that He gave His one and only Son. Anyone who believes in Him will not die but will have eternal life (John 3:16).

+ People who don't believe might say you are doing wrong. But lead good lives among them. Then they will see your good works. And they will give glory to God on the day He comes to judge (1 Peter 2:12).

FEAR

+ When you lie down you will not be afraid. When you lie down your sleep will be sweet (Proverbs 3:24).

+ Take good care of me, just as You would take care of Your own eyes. Hide me in the shadow of Your wings (Psalm 17:8).

+ God didn't give us a spirit that makes us weak and fearful. He gave us a spirit that gives us power and love. It helps us control ourselves (2 Timothy 1:7).

+ The LORD is the one who keeps you safe. So let the Most High God be like a home to you. Then no harm will come to you. No terrible plague will come near your tent (Psalm 91:9-10).

FRIENDSHIPS

+ People who don't believe might say you are doing wrong. But lead good lives among them. Then they will see your good works. And they will give glory to God on the day He comes to judge (1 Peter 2:12).

+ A friend loves at all times. He is there to help when trouble comes (Proverbs 17:17).

+ If you love one another, everyone will know you are My disciples (John 13:35).

+ Do two people walk together unless they've agreed to do so? (Amos 3:3)

+ Here is My command. Love each other (John 15:17).

+ How good and pleasant it is when God's people live together in peace (Psalm 133)!

FAMILY

+ God gives lonely people a family. He sets prisoners free, and they go out singing. But those who refuse to obey Him live in a land that is baked by the sun (Psalm 68:6).

+ I will teach parents how to love their children and will also teach children how to honor their parents (Malachi 4:6).

+ Children, obey your parents in the Lord, for this is right. "Honor your father and mother"—which is the first commandment with a promise—"that it may go well with you and that you may enjoy long life on the earth" (Ephesians 6:1-3).

+ Fathers, don't make your children angry. Instead, train them and teach them the ways of the Lord as you raise them (Ephesians 6:4).

+ Children, obey your parents in everything, for this pleases the Lord. Fathers, don't make your children bitter. If you do, they will lose hope (Colossians 3:20-21).

SAFETY

+ I will lie down in peace and sleep, for You alone, O Lord, will keep me safe (Psalm 4:8).

+ Because you trusted Me, I will preserve your life and keep you safe. I, the Lord, have spoken (Jeremiah 39:18)!

+ The Lord is a place of safety for those who have been beaten down. He keeps them safe in times of trouble (Psalm 9:9).

+ You have not handed me over to my enemy but have set me in a safe place (Psalm 31:8).

+ The name of the Lord is like a strong tower. Godly people run to it and are safe (Proverbs 18:10).

+ I do not pray that You will take them out of the world. I pray that You will keep them safe from the evil one (John 17:15).

OBEDIENCE

+ I will never forget Your rules. You have kept me alive, because I obey them (Psalm 119:93).

+ Children, obey your parents in the Lord, for this is right (Ephesians 6:1).

+ He replied, "Instead, blessed are those who hear God's word and obey it"   (Luke 11:23).

LOVING OTHERS

+ Lord, who can live in Your sacred tent? Who can stay on your Holy hill? He doesn't tell lies about others. He doesn't do wrong to His neighbors. He doesn't say anything bad about them. He hates sinful people. He honors those who have respect for the Lord. He keeps His promises even when it hurts (Psalm. 15:1,3-4).

+ Dear friends, let us love one another, because love comes from God. Everyone who loves has been born again because of what God has done. That person knows God (1 John 4:7).

+ Dear children, don't just talk about love. Put your love into action. Then it will truly be love (1 John 3:18).

+ But here is what I tell you. Love your enemies. Pray for those who hurt you. Then you will be sons of your Father who is in heaven. He causes His sun to shine on evil people and good people. He sends rain on those who do right and those who don't (Matthew 5:44-45).

+ Finally, I want all of you to live together in peace. Be understanding. Love one another like members of the same family. Be kind and tender. Don't be proud (1 Peter 3:8).

+ If you love one another, everyone will know you are My disciples (John 13:35).

UNITY WITH FAMILY AND FRIENDS

+ If you are pure and live with complete integrity, He will rise up and restore your happy home (Job 8:6).

+ Don't be proud at all. Be completely gentle. Be patient. Put up with one another in love. The Holy Spirit makes you one in everyway. So try your best to remain as one. Let peace keep you together (Ephesians 4:2-3).

+ All the believers were agreed in heart and mind. They didn't claim that anything they had was their own. They shared everything they owned (Acts 4:32).

+ Then make my joy complete by agreeing with each other. Have the same love. Be one in spirit and purpose (Philippians 2:2).

DAILY WALKING THROUGH THE WORD

All Scripture is given by inspiration of God, and is profitable for doctrine, for reproof, for correction, for instruction in righteousness, that the man of God may be complete, thoroughly equipped for every good work (2 Timothy 3:16-17).

Inductive Bible Study: As you study the Word, use these Inductive Bible Study guidelines to help you better understand what each passage of scripture is saying, what it means, and how to apply it.

> **INVESTIGATION:** Investigation teaches you to see exactly what the passage says. It is the basis for accurate interpretation and correct application. Investigation answers the question, "What does the passage say?"
>
> **INTERPRETATION:** While investigation leads to an accurate understanding of what the Word of God says, interpretation goes a step further and helps you understand what it means in the context in which it was written.
>
> **APPLICATION:** The first step in application is to find out what the Word of God says on any particular subject through accurate and correct interpretation of the text. Once you understand what the Word of God teaches, you then obey the truths by applying them to your life.

WALKING THROUGH THE WORD PODCAST

Walk through the word with New Song Nashville's devotional commentary from the depths of the Scriptures. If you have been challenged in knowing how to apply the truths that are buried in the Word to your life, listen for an overview of the daily Old Testament and New Testament readings and a central theme with some helpful points of application.

To access, search in your mobile app for "Walking Through The Word Podcast" or go to newsongnashville.com and click on the podcast icon at the bottom of the page.

REACH IN TO ONE ANOTHER
through the ministries of making disciples, developing leaders and multiplying covenantal community

REACH IN
MAKING DISCIPLES, DEVELOPTING LEADERS & MULTIPLYING COVENANTAL COMMUNITY

MAKING DISCIPLES: And Jesus came and spoke to them, saying, "All authority has been given to Me in heaven and on earth. Go therefore and make disciples of all the nations, baptizing them in the name of the Father and of the Son and of the Holy Spirit, teaching them to observe all things that I have commanded you; and lo, I am with you always, even to the end of the age." Amen (Matthew 28:18-20).

DEVELOPING LEADERS: And the things that you have heard from me among many witnesses, commit these to faithful men who will be able to teach others also (2 Timothy 2:2).

MULTIPLYING COVENANTAL COMMUNITY: And let us consider one another in order to stir up love and good works, not forsaking the assembling of ourselves together, as is the manner of some, but exhorting one another, and so much the more as you see the day approaching (Hebrews 10:24-25).

LIFE REACH SCHOOL OF MINISTRY

Life Reach School of Ministry provides a context for our New Song family to lovingly serve and equip one another to reach our full potential in Christ at every age and every stage. We accomplish this by discipling to Christ, mentoring to task, and coaching to excellence.

Life Reach School of Ministry Includes:

- Age-Based Discipling
- Life Groups
- Equipping Groups
- Leadership Training
- Topic-focused Seminars
- Resources and Publications

REACH OUT TO THE WORLD

through the ministries of
evangelism, compassion
and justice.

REACH OUT
EVANGELISM, COMPASSION & JUSTICE

EVANGELISM: And [Jesus] said to them,"Go into all the world and preach the gospel to every creature. He who believes and is baptized will be saved; but he who does not believe will be condemned" (Mark 16:15-16).

COMPASSION & JUSTICE: Thus says the Lord of hosts: "Execute true justice, show mercy and compassion everyone to his brother" (Zechariah 7:9).

THE GOSPEL CREED

The GOSPEL is the GOOD NEWS that God became man in Jesus Christ. He lived the life we should have lived and died the death we should have died—in our place. Three days later He rose from the dead, proving that He is the Son of God and offering the gift of salvation and forgiveness of sins to everyone who repents and believes in Him.

WHY SHOULD I PUT MY FAITH IN CHRIST?

+ **We have a human problem.** We are separated from a perfect and holy God because all of man is in a state of spiritual death. Evil is not just an entity that exists in our world, it is also in us. Because of this, we are drawn to works of darkness—all manner of sin and deception. "For all have sinned and fall short of the glory of God" (Romans 3:23). Sin's penalty is an eternity spent in hell separated from God.

+ **All of our own efforts fall short** of what God requires in order to be in relationship with Him. Our desperate need is for a completely transformed heart that pursues good and not evil; we also need forgiveness and pardon of our sins. We are utterly helpless, unable to save ourselves.

+ **So we need reconciliation**—a bridge between us and God. The Bible tells us that God so loved the world that He gave His one and only Son Jesus to be the sacrifice for our sins; Jesus paid our penalty in full when He died on the cross (see John 3:13-18). God, through Christ Jesus, has made a way for us to be back in right relationship with Him. "For the wages of sin is death, but the free gift of God is eternal life in Christ Jesus our Lord" (Romans 6:23).

+ **Jesus Christ is our bridge to God.** In John 14:6, Jesus says; "I am the way, the truth, and the life. No one comes to the Father except through Me." By repenting of our own sin and rebellion against God, believing in Christ's sacrifice for our sin, and confessing Jesus as Lord, we can be saved from the penalty of sin and reconciled to God. Romans 10:9 says, "If you confess with your mouth the Lord Jesus and believe in your heart that God has raised Him from the dead, you will be saved."

+ **Then a miracle happens!** God is faithful to forgive our sins, give us a clean slate and a new, transformed heart, and welcome us into relationship with Him.

+ **The next step is to confess your sins.** Are you willing to follow Jesus and trust Him with your life? As you pray, confess any cyclical sin, addictions, etc., that God by His Holy Spirit brings to your mind. You can let it all go!

A PRAYER OF SALVATION:

"Heavenly Father, I thank You for Your love for me and for the gift of Your Son, Jesus, to die for all who have sinned. I confess that I have broken Your laws and sinned against You and am in desperate need of a Savior. I now turn away from my sin and turn to You, and I put my faith and trust in Jesus and His work on the cross, where He died in my place and was then raised from the dead that I might have new life in Him. I ask You to forgive me of my sins and give me eternal life. I realize that You forgive me, not because of anything I've done, but because of Jesus' sacrifice and my faith and trust in His work alone. Help me now to grow in intimacy with You and Your Word, and give me a heart to share Your love and forgiveness with others. In Jesus' name, Amen."

Praise God!
All of heaven rejoices with you today!

"Likewise, I say to you, there is joy in the presence of the angels of God over one sinner who repents" (Luke 15:10).

YOUR NEXT STEPS AS A DISCIPLE (FOLLOWER) OF CHRIST:

Share
Tell others what He has done for you! Jesus just saved you from eternity in hell and separation from your loving Heavenly Father; this is GOOD NEWS! "And He died for all, that those who live should live no longer for themselves, but for Him who died for them and rose again" (2 Corinthians 5:15).

Pray
You have just entered into the most important relationship of your life. Make talking and listening to God a high priority. He wants to spend time with you!

Read
The Bible is God's living word. God speaks to us through it, and He calls us to obey what He says by His Spirit. Believe every word you read! "For the word of God is full of living power. It is sharper than the sharpest knife, cutting deep into our innermost thoughts and desires. It exposes us for what we really are" (Hebrews 4:6).

Connect
You need a Bible-believing church to help you learn about God and find others who believe what you believe and will help you grow as a disciple of Christ. "God places the lonely in families; He sets the prisoners free and gives them joy" (Psalm 68:6).

MissionTEN.8

We are committed, over the 2010-2019 decade, to seeing ten years of the greatest ministry we have ever known. We believe during this "Decade of the King" we will see a ten-year stretch of time where King Jesus is glorified in the earth in an unparalleled way in our experience as we serve Jesus by serving the needs of people in our community, in our state, our nation and in our world. MissionTEN.8 is the eighth year of this "Decade of the King," where New Song is committed to the following areas:

+ **Personal Evangelism:** Job #1 for us is to get out into the harvest field of our community and lead lost people to Christ. God has called us to reach those within our reach by the declaration and demonstration of the Gospel of the Kingdom wherever we go and in whatever places God sends us. Paul teaches us in Romans 1:16-17 not to be ashamed of the gospel because "it is the power of God to salvation for everyone who believes." We believe God is calling all of us to share the gospel personally and powerfully with every person in our spheres of influence.

+ **Multiplication of Covenantal Community:** Multiplying covenantal communities is one of our New Song ministry values and is the heart of what we are doing to reach our city for Christ. Rather than just being a "come-to" church, it is our goal to be a "go-to" church to more effectively and personally reach people where they are through the multiplication of covenantal communities such as Life Groups, Equipping Groups, discipleship groups, and more throughout the Greater Nashville area. By doing this, the people of New Song are in their communities close to the needs and are ready, willing and able to meet those needs. We believe this is our most effective way to get out and into the lives of the most people possible.

+ **Community Partners:** We believe it is vital to seek both to know the needs of our community and to meet those needs, and in the process, to share the life and light of Jesus Christ. Community Partners are ministries of compassion and justice with whom we serve the needs in our community while sharing the good news of Jesus Christ's love and power. We have made a commitment to serve and bless our community by establishing and strengthening covenantal relationships with local ministry partners.

+ **Global Partners:** God has given us global assignments with specific peoples and nations where we are to advance His Kingdom with His good news, love and power. In 2018 we will continue to focus on our Strategic Global Assignments— Dominican Republic, India, Mexico, Kenya and Nepal— in addition to other projects locally and globally. To do this, we walk in covenantal relationship with missionaries serving in the nations, and we are committed to helping them have the resources they need to accomplish the tasks that God has given them.

+ **GOTeams:** We are called to make an indelible mark for the gospel as we partner with missionaries around the world by going and helping them strengthen ministry that is permanent and ongoing. We will send short-term Gospel Outreach Teams (GOTeams) in response to the needs of our Global Partners, providing an opportunity for members of New Song to serve in the nations around the globe. In so doing, we commit to learn, love and serve everywhere our teams go to impact the nations for His Kingdom.

HELP US REACH OUR FINANCIAL GOAL FOR MISSIONTEN.8! HERE'S HOW:

- Mail your contributions to: New Song MissionTEN.8
  316 Southgate Court // Brentwood TN 37027
- Give online: NewSongNashville.com
- Put your contribution in the MissionTEN.8 basket at church on Sunday

PERSONAL VISION & GOALS

Take some time to pray and ask the Lord to reveal through His Holy Spirit what His vision and goals are for you in this coming season, and write them down. Share them with a few trusted friends and leaders, and pray into them regularly.

Spiritual | I will instruct you and teach you in the way you should go; I will guide you with My eye (Psalm 32:8).

_____

_____

_____

_____

_____

_____

_____

Personal | For we are His workmanship, created in Christ Jesus for good works, which God prepared beforehand that we should walk in them. (Ephesians 2:10).

_____

_____

_____

_____

_____

_____

_____

Educational | Happy is the man who finds wisdom, and the man who gains understanding (Proverbs 3:13).

_____

_____

_____

_____

_____

_____

_____

_____

_____

_____

Relational | By this all will know that you are My disciples, if you have love for one another (John 13:35).

_____

_____

_____

_____

_____

_____

_____

_____

_____

_____

Personal
Vision
& Goals

Health & Fitness | Or do you not know that your body
is the temple of the Holy Spirit who is in you, whom you have from
God, and you are not your own? For you were bought at a price;
therefore glorify God in your body and in your spirit, which are God's
(1 Corinthians 6:19-20).

_____

_____

_____

_____

_____

_____

_____

_____

_____

_____

Financial | The generous soul will be made rich, and he
who waters will also be watered himself (Proverbs 11:25).

_____

_____

_____

_____

_____

_____

_____

_____

_____

_____

Personal
Vision
& Goals

Home & Family | And if it seems evil to you to serve the Lord, choose for yourselves this day whom you will serve, whether the gods which your fathers served that were on the other side of the River, or the gods of the Amorites, in whose land you dwell. But as for me and my house, we will serve the Lord (Joshua 24:15).

_____

_____

_____

_____

_____

_____

_____

_____

_____

Ministry | And He said to them, "Go into all the world and preach the gospel to every creature..." (Mark 16:15).

_____

_____

_____

_____

_____

_____

_____

_____

_____

JANUARY 2018

	Old Testament	New Testament	Psalms	Proverbs
1	Gen 1:1-2:25	Matt 1:1-2:12	1:1-6	1:1-6
2	Gen 3:1-4:26	Matt 2:13-3:6	2:1-12	1:7-9
3	Gen 5:1-7:24	Matt 3:7-4:11	3:1-8	1:10-19
4	Gen 8:1-10:32	Matt 4:12-25	4:1-8	1:20-23
5	Gen 11:1-12:20	Matt 5:1-26	5:1-12	1:24-28
6	Gen 13:1-15:21	Matt 5:27-48	6:1-10	1:29-33
7	Gen 16:1-18:15	Matt 6:1-24	7:1-17	2:1-5
8	Gen 18:16-19:38	Matt 6:25-7:14	8:1-9	2:6-15
9	Gen 20:1-22:24	Matt 7:15-29	9:1-10	2:16-22
10	Gen 23:1-24:67	Matt 8:1-17	9:11-20	3:1-6
11	Gen 25:1-26:17	Matt 8:18-34	10:1-7	3:7-8
12	Gen 26:18-27:46	Matt 9:1-17	10:8-18	3:9-10
13	Gen 28:1-29:35	Matt 9:18-38	11:1-7	3:11-12
14	Gen 30:1-31:21	Matt 10:1-26	12:1-8	3:13-15
15	Gen 31:22-32:12	Matt 10:27-11:6	13:1-6	3:16-18
16	Gen 32:13-34:31	Matt 11:7-30	14:1-7	3:19-20
17	Gen 35:1-36:43	Matt 12:1-21	15:1-5	3:21-26
18	Gen 37:1-38:30	Matt 12:22-45	16:1-11	3:27-32
19	Gen 39:1-41:16	Matt 12:46-13:23	17:1-15	3:33-35
20	Gen 41:17-42:17	Matt 13:24-46	18:1-15	4:1-6
21	Gen 42:18-43:34	Matt 13:47-14:12	18:16-34	4:7-9
22	Gen 44:1-45:28	Matt 14:13-36	18:35-50	4:10-13
23	Gen 46:1-47:31	Matt 15:1-28	19:1-14	4:14-19
24	Gen 48:1-49:33	Matt 15:29-16:12	20:1-9	4:20-27
25	Gen 50:1-Ex 2:10	Matt 16:13-17:9	21:1-13	5:1-6
26	Ex 2:11-3:22	Matt 17:10-27	22:1-15	5:7-14
27	Ex 4:1-5:21	Matt 18:1-20	22:16-31	5:15-21
28	Ex 5:22-7:25	Matt 18:21-19:12	23:1-6	5:22-23
29	Ex 8:1-9:35	Matt 19:13-30	24:1-10	6:1-5
30	Ex 10:1-12:13	Matt 20:1-28	25:1-11	6:6-11
31	Ex 12:14-13:16	Matt 20:29-21:22	25:12-22	6:12-15

KEY PASSAGES:

_____
_____
_____
_____
_____
_____
_____
_____
_____

PRAYER REQUESTS:

Date:	Request:	Date Answered:

JANUARY 2018

Sunday	Monday	Tuesday	Wednesday
	1 New Year's Day	2	3
7	8	9	10
14	15 Martin Luther King, Jr.	16	17
21	22	23	24
28	29	30	31

Thursday	Friday	Saturday	Notes
4	5	6	
11	12	13	
18	19	20	
25	26	27	

FEBRUARY 2018

	Old Testament	New Testament	Psalms	Proverbs
1	Ex 13:17-15:19	Matt 21:23-46	26:1-12	6:16-19
2	Ex 15:20-17:7	Matt 22:1-33	27:1-6	6:20-26
3	Ex 17:8-19:15	Matt 22:34-23:12	27:7-14	6:27-35
4	Ex 19:16-21:27	Matt 23:13-39	28:1-9	7:1-5
5	Ex 21:28-23:13	Matt 24:1-28	29:1-11	7:6-23
6	Ex 23:14-25:40	Matt 24:29-51	30:1-12	7:24-27
7	Ex 26:1-27:21	Matt 25:1-30	31:1-8	8:1-11
8	Ex 28:1-43	Matt 25:31-26:13	31:9-18	8:12-13
9	Ex 29:1-30:10	Matt 26:14-46	31:19-24	8:14-26
10	Ex 30:11-31:18	Matt 26:47-68	32:1-11	8:27-31
11	Ex 32:1-33:23	Matt 26:69-27:14	33:1-12	8:32-36
12	Ex 34:1-35:9	Matt 27:15-37	33:13-22	9:1-6
13	Ex 35:10-36:38	Matt 27:38-66	34:1-10	9:7-8
14	Ex 37:1-38:31	Matt 28:1-20	34:11-22	9:9-10
15	Ex 39:1-40:38	Mark 1:1-28	35:1-16	9:11-12
16	Lev 1:1-3:17	Mark 1:29-2:12	35:17-28	9:13-18
17	Lev 4:1-5:19	Mark 2:13-3:6	36:1-12	10:1-2
18	Lev 6:1-7:27	Mark 3:7-30	37:1-11	10:3-4
19	Lev 7:28-9:6	Mark 3:31-4:25	37:12-28	10:5
20	Lev 9:7-10:20	Mark 4:26-5:20	37:29-40	10:6-7
21	Lev 11:1-12:8	Mark 5:21-43	38:1-22	10:8-9
22	Lev 13:1-59	Mark 6:1-29	39:1-13	10:10
23	Lev 14:1-57	Mark 6:30-56	40:1-10	10:11-12
24	Lev 15:1-16:34	Mark 7:1-23	40:11-17	10:13-14
25	Lev 17:1-18:30	Mark 7:24-8:10	41:1-13	10:15
26	Lev 19:1-20:21	Mark 8:11-38	42:1-11	10:16
27	Lev 20:22-22:16	Mark 9:1-29	43:1-5	10:17
28	Lev 22:17-23:44	Mark 9:30-10:12	44:1-12	10:18-19

KEY PASSAGES:

_____
_____
_____
_____
_____
_____
_____
_____
_____
_____

PRAYER REQUESTS:

Date:	Request:	Date Answered:

FEBRUARY 2018

Sunday	Monday	Tuesday	Wednesday
4	5	6	7
11	12	13	14 Valentine's Day
18	19 President's Day	20	21
25	26	27	28

Thursday	Friday	Saturday	Notes
1	2	3	
8	9	10	
15	16	17	
22	23	24	

MARCH 2018

	Old Testament	New Testament	Psalms	Proverbs
1	Lev 24:1-25:46	Mark 10:13-31	44:13-26	10:20-21
2	Lev 25:47-27:13	Mark 10:32-52	45:1-17	10:22
3	Lev 27:14-Num 1:54	Mark 11:1-26	46:1-11	10:23
4	Num 2:1-3:51	Mark 11:27-12:17	47:1-9	10:24-25
5	Num 4:1-5:31	Mark 12:18-37	48:1-14	10:26
6	Num 6:1-7:89	Mark 12:38-13:13	49:1-20	10:27-28
7	Num 8:1-9:23	Mark 13:14-37	50:1-23	10:29-30
8	Num 10:1-11:23	Mark 14:1-21	51:1-19	10:31-32
9	Num 11:24-13:33	Mark 14:22-52	52:1-9	11:1-3
10	Num 14:1-15:21	Mark 14:53-72	53:1-6	11:4
11	Num 15:22-16:40	Mark 15:1-47	54:1-7	11:5-6
12	Num 16:41-18:32	Mark 16:1-20	55:1-23	11:7
13	Num 19:1-20:29	Luke 1:1-25	56:1-13	11:8
14	Num 21:1-22:21	Luke 1:26-56	57:1-11	11:9-11
15	Num 22:22-23:30	Luke 1:57-80	58:1-11	11:12-13
16	Num 24:1-25:18	Luke 2:1-35	59:1-17	11:14
17	Num 26:1-51	Luke 2:36-52	60:1-12	11:15
18	Num 26:52-28:15	Luke 3:1-22	61:1-8	11:16-17
19	Num 28:16-29:40	Luke 3:23-38	62:1-12	11:18-19
20	Num 30:1-31:54	Luke 4:1-30	63:1-11	11:20-21
21	Num 32:1-33:39	Luke 4:31-5:11	64:1-10	11:22
22	Num 33:40-35:34	Luke 5:12-26	65:1-13	11:23
23	Num 36:1-Deut 1:46	Luke 5:27-6:11	66:1-20	11:24-26
24	Deut 2:1-3:29	Luke 6:12-36	67:1-7	11:27
25	Deut 4:1-49	Luke 6:37-7:10	68:1-18	11:28
26	Deut 5:1-6:25	Luke 7:11-35	68:19-35	11:29-31
27	Deut 7:1-8:20	Luke 7:36-8:3	69:1-18	12:1
28	Deut 9:1-10:22	Luke 8:4-21	69:19-36	12:2-3
29	Deut 11:1-12:32	Luke 8:22-39	70:1-5	12:4
30	Deut 13:1-15:23	Luke 8:40-9:6	71:1-24	12:5-7
31	Deut 16:1-17:20	Luke 9:7-27	72:1-20	12:8-9

KEY PASSAGES:

_____
_____
_____
_____
_____
_____
_____
_____
_____

PRAYER REQUESTS:

Date:	Request:	Date Answered:

MARCH 2018

Sunday	Monday	Tuesday	Wednesday
4	5	6	7
11 Daylight Saving (Start)	12	13	14
18	19	20	21
25	26	27	28

Thursday	Friday	Saturday	Notes
1	2	3	
8	9	10	
15	16	17 St. Patrick's Day	
22	23	24	
29	30 Good Friday	31	

APRIL 2018

	Old Testament	New Testament	Psalms	Proverbs
1	Deut 18:1-20:20	Luke 9:28-50	73:1-28	12:10
2	Deut 21:1-22:30	Luke 9:51-10:12	74:1-23	12:11
3	Deut 23:1-25:19	Luke 10:13-37	75:1-10	12:12-14
4	Deut 26:1-27:26	Luke 10:38-11:13	76:1-12	12:15-17
5	Deut 28:1-68	Luke 11:14-36	77:1-20	12:18
6	Deut 29:1-30:20	Luke 11:37-12:7	78:1-25	12:19-20
7	Deut 31:1-32:9	Luke 12:8-34	78:26-45	12:21-23
8	Deut 32:10-52	Luke 12:35-59	78:46-55	12:24
9	Deut 33:1-29	Luke 13:1-21	78:56-72	12:25
10	Deut 34:1-Josh 2:24	Luke 13:22-14:6	79:1-13	12:26
11	Josh 3:1-4:24	Luke 14:7-35	80:1-19	12:27-28
12	Josh 5:1-7:15	Luke 15:1-32	81:1-16	13:1
13	Josh 7:16-8:35	Luke 16:1-18	82:1-8	13:2-3
14	Josh 9:1-10:43	Luke 16:19-17:10	83:1-18	13:4
15	Josh 11:1-12:24	Luke 17:11-37	84:1-12	13:5-6
16	Josh 13:1-14:15	Luke 18:1-17	85:1-13	13:7-8
17	Josh 15:1-63	Luke 18:18-43	86:1-17	13:9-10
18	Josh 16:1-18:28	Luke 19:1-27	87:1-7	13:11
19	Josh 19:1-20:9	Luke 19:28-48	88:1-18	13:12-14
20	Josh 21:1-22:20	Luke 20:1-26	89:1-18	13:15-16
21	Josh 22:21-23:16	Luke 20:27-47	89:19-37	13:17-19
22	Josh 24:1-33	Luke 21:1-28	89:38-52	13:20-23
23	Judges 1:1-2:10	Luke 21:29-22:13	90:1-91:16	13:24-25
24	Judges 2:11-3:31	Luke 22:14-34	92:1-93:5	14:1-2
25	Judges 4:1-5:31	Luke 22:35-53	94:1-23	14:3-4
26	Judges 6:1-40	Luke 22:54-23:12	95:1-96:13	14:5-6
27	Judges 7:1-8:16	Luke 23:13-43	97:1-98:9	14:7-8
28	Judges 8:17-9:21	Luke 23:44-24:12	99:1-9	14:9-10
29	Judges 9:22-10:18	Luke 24:13-53	100:1-5	14:11-12
30	Judges 11:1-12:15	John 1:1-28	101:1-8	14:13-14

KEY PASSAGES:

_____
_____
_____
_____
_____
_____
_____
_____
_____
_____

PRAYER REQUESTS:

Date:	Request:	Date Answered:

APRIL 2018

Sunday	Monday	Tuesday	Wednesday
1 Easter	2	3	4
8	9	10	11
15	16	17	18
22	23	24	25
29	30		

Thursday	Friday	Saturday	Notes
5	6	7	
12	13	14	
19	20	21	
26	27	28	

MAY 2018

	Old Testament	New Testament	Psalms	Proverbs
1	Judges 13:1-14:20	John 1:29-51	102:1-28	14:15-16
2	Judges 15:1-16:31	John 2:1-25	103:1-22	14:17-19
3	Judges 17:1-18:31	John 3:1-21	104:1-18	14:20-21
4	Judges 19:1-20:48	John 3:22-4:4	104:19-35	14:22-24
5	Judges 21:1-Ruth 1:22	John 4:5-42	105:1-15	14:25
6	Ruth 2:1-4:22	John 4:43-54	105:16-36	14:26-27
7	I Sam 1:1-2:21	John 5:1-23	105:37-45	14:28-29
8	I Sam 2:22-4:22	John 5:24-47	106:1-23	14:30-31
9	I Sam 5:1-7:17	John 6:1-21	106:24-48	14:32-33
10	I Sam 8:1-9:26	John 6:22-40	107:1-16	14:34-35
11	I Sam 9:27-11:15	John 6:41-71	107:17-43	15:1-3
12	I Sam 12:1-13:23	John 7:1-24	108:1-13	15:4
13	I Sam 14:1-52	John 7:25-8:1	109:1-31	15:5-7
14	I Sam 15:1-16:23	John 8:2-20	110:1-7	15:8-10
15	I Sam 17:1-18:4	John 8:21-36	111:1-10	15:11
16	I Sam 18:5-19:24	John 8:37-59	112:1-10	15:12-14
17	I Sam 20:1-21:15	John 9:1-41	113:1-114:8	15:15-17
18	I Sam 22:1-23:29	John 10:1-21	115:1-18	15:18-19
19	I Sam 24:1-25:44	John 10:22-42	116:1-19	15:20-21
20	I Sam 26:1-28:25	John 11:1-54	117:1-2	15:22-23
21	I Sam 29:1-31:13	John 11:55-12:19	118:1-18	15:24-26
22	II Sam 1:1-2:11	John 12:20-50	118:19-29	15:27-28
23	II Sam 2:12-3:39	John 13:1-30	119:1-16	15:29-30
24	II Sam 4:1-6:23	John 13:31-14:18	119:17-32	15:31-32
25	II Sam 7:1-8:18	John 14:19-31	119:33-48	15:33
26	II Sam 9:1-11:27	John 15:1-27	119:49-64	16:1-3
27	II Sam 12:1-31	John 16:1-33	119:65-80	16:4-5
28	II Sam 13:1-39	John 17:1-26	119:81-96	16:6-7
29	II Sam 14:1-15:18	John 18:1-24	119:97-112	16:8-9
30	II Sam 15:19-16:23	John 18:25-19:24	119:113-128	16:10-11
31	II Sam 17:1-29	John 19:25-42	119:129-152	16:12-13

KEY PASSAGES:

_____
_____
_____
_____
_____
_____
_____
_____
_____

PRAYER REQUESTS:

Date:	Request:	Date Answered:

MAY 2018

Sunday	Monday	Tuesday	Wednesday
		1	2
6	7	8	9
13 Mother's Day	14	15	16
20 Pentecost	21	22	23
27	28 Memorial Day	29	30

Thursday	Friday	Saturday	Notes
3 National Day of Prayer	4	5 Cinco de Mayo	
10	11	12	
17	18	19	
24	25	26	
31			

JUNE 2018

	Old Testament	New Testament	Psalms	Proverbs
1	II Sam 18:1-19:8	John 20:1-31	119:153-176	16:14-15
2	II Sam 19:9-20:14	John 21:1-25	120:1-7	16:16-17
3	II Sam 20:15-22:20	Acts 1:1-26	121:1-8	16:18
4	II Sam 22:21-23:23	Acts 2:1-47	122:1-9	16:19-20
5	II Sam 23:24-24:25	Acts 3:1-26	123:1-4	16:21-23
6	I Kings 1:1-53	Acts 4:1-37	124:1-8	16:24
7	I Kings 2:1-46	Acts 5:1-42	125:1-5	16:25
8	I Kings 3:1-4:34	Acts 6:1-15	126:1-6	16:26-27
9	I Kings 5:1-6:38	Acts 7:1-29	127:1-5	16:28-30
10	I Kings 7:1-51	Acts 7:30-50	128:1-6	16:31-33
11	I Kings 8:1-66	Acts 7:51-8:13	129:1-8	17:1
12	I Kings 9:1-10:29	Acts 8:14-40	130:1-8	17:2-3
13	I Kings 11:1-12:19	Acts 9:1-25	131:1-3	17:4-5
14	I Kings 12:20-13:34	Acts 9:26-43	132:1-18	17:6
15	I Kings 14:1-15:24	Acts 10:1-23	133:1-3	17:7-8
16	I Kings 15:25-17:24	Acts 10:24-48	134:1-3	17:9-11
17	I Kings 18:1-46	Acts 11:1-30	135:1-21	17:12-13
18	I Kings 19:1-21	Acts 12:1-24	136:1-26	17:14-15
19	I Kings 20:1-21:29	Acts 12:25-13:12	137:1-9	17:16
20	I Kings 22:1-53	Acts 13:13-41	138:1-8	17:17-18
21	II Kings 1:1-2:25	Acts 13:42-14:7	139:1-24	17:19-21
22	II Kings 3:1-4:17	Acts 14:8-28	140:1-13	17:22
23	II Kings 4:18-5:27	Acts 15:1-29	141:1-10	17:23
24	II Kings 6:1-7:20	Acts 15:30-16:15	142:1-7	17:24-25
25	II Kings 8:1-9:13	Acts 16:16-40	143:1-12	17:26
26	II Kings 9:14-10:31	Acts 17:1-34	144:1-15	17:27-28
27	II Kings 10:32-12:21	Acts 18:1-23	145:1-21	18:1
28	II Kings 13:1-14:29	Acts 18:24-19:10	146:1-10	18:2-3
29	II Kings 15:1-16:20	Acts 19:11-41	147:1-20	18:4-5
30	II Kings 17:1-18:16	Acts 20:1-38	148:1-14	18:6-7

KEY PASSAGES:

_____
_____
_____
_____
_____
_____
_____
_____
_____
_____

PRAYER REQUESTS:

Date:	Request:	Date Answered:

JUNE 2018

Sunday	Monday	Tuesday	Wednesday
3	4	5	6
10	11	12	13
17 Father's Day	18	19	20
24	25	26	27

Thursday	Friday	Saturday	Notes
	1	2	
7	8	9	
14	15	16	
21	22	23	
28	29	30	

JULY 2018

	Old Testament	New Testament	Psalms	Proverbs
1	II Kings 18:17-19:37	Acts 21:1-14	149:1-9	18:8
2	II Kings 20:1-22:2	Acts 21:15-36	150:1-6	18:9-10
3	II Kings 22:3-23:30	Acts 21:37-22:16	1:1-6	18:11-12
4	II Kings 23:31-25:30	Acts 22:17-23:10	2:1-12	18:13
5	I Chron 1:1-2:17	Acts 23:11-35	3:1-8	18:14-15
6	I Chron 2:18-4:8	Acts 24:1-27	4:1-8	18:16-18
7	I Chron 4:9-5:10	Acts 25:1-27	5:1-12	18:19
8	I Chron 5:11-6:81	Acts 26:1-32	6:1-10	18:20-21
9	I Chron 7:1-8:40	Acts 27:1-20	7:1-17	18:22
10	I Chron 9:1-10:14	Acts 27:21-44	8:1-9	18:23-24
11	I Chron 11:1-12:22	Acts 28:1-31	9:1-10	19:1-3
12	I Chron 12:23-14:17	Rom 1:1-17	9:11-20	19:4-5
13	I Chron 15:1-16:36	Rom 1:18-32	10:1-7	19:6-7
14	I Chron 16:37-18:17	Rom 2:1-24	10:8-18	19:8-9
15	I Chron 19:1-21:30	Rom 2:25-3:8	11:1-7	19:10-12
16	I Chron 22:1-23:32	Rom 3:9-31	12:1-8	19:13-14
17	I Chron 24:1-26:11	Rom 4:1-12	13:1-6	19:15-16
18	I Chron 26:12-27:34	Rom 4:13-5:2	14:1-7	19:17
19	I Chron 28:1-29:30	Rom 5:3-21	15:1-5	19:18-19
20	II Chron 1:1-3:17	Rom 6:1-23	16:1-11	19:20-21
21	II Chron 4:1-6:11	Rom 7:1-13	17:1-15	19:22-23
22	II Chron 6:12-8:10	Rom 7:13-8:11	18:1-15	19:24-25
23	II Chron 8:11-10:19	Rom 8:12-25	18:16-34	19:26
24	II Chron 11:1-13:22	Rom 8:26-39	18:35-50	19:27-29
25	II Chron 14:1-16:14	Rom 9:1-24	19:1-14	20:1
26	II Chron 17:1-18:34	Rom 9:25-10:13	20:1-9	20:2-3
27	II Chron 19:1-20:37	Rom 10:14-11:10	21:1-13	20:4-6
28	II Chron 21:1-23:21	Rom 11:11-36	22:1-15	20:07
29	II Chron 24:1-25:28	Rom 12:1-21	22:16-31	20:8-10
30	II Chron 26:1-28:27	Rom 13:1-14	23:1-6	20:11
31	II Chron 29:1-36	Rom 14:1-23	24:1-10	20:12

KEY PASSAGES:

_____
_____
_____
_____
_____
_____
_____
_____
_____
_____

PRAYER REQUESTS:

Date:	Request:	Date Answered:

JULY 2018

Sunday	Monday	Tuesday	Wednesday
1	2	3	4 Independence Day
8	9	10	11
15	16	17	18
22	23	24	25
29	30	31	

Thursday	Friday	Saturday	Notes
5	6	7	
12	13	14	
19	20	21	
26	27	28	

AUGUST 2018

	Old Testament	New Testament	Psalms	Proverbs
1	II Chron 30:1-31:21	Rom 15:1-21	25:1-11	20:13-15
2	II Chron 32:1-33:9	Rom 15:22-16:7	25:12-22	20:16-18
3	II Chron 33:10-34:33	Rom 16:8-27	26:1-12	20:19
4	II Chron 35:1-36:23	I Cor 1:1-17	27:1-6	20:20-21
5	Ezra 1:1-2:70	I Cor 1:18-2:5	27:7-14	20:22-23
6	Ezra 3:1-4:24	I Cor 2:6-3:4	28:1-9	20:24-25
7	Ezra 5:1-6:22	I Cor 3:5-23	29:1-11	20:26-27
8	Ezra 7:1-8:20	I Cor 4:1-21	30:1-12	20:28-30
9	Ezra 8:21-9:15	I Cor 5:1-13	31:1-8	21:1-2
10	Ezra 10:1-44	I Cor 6:1-20	31:9-18	21:3
11	Neh 1:1-3:14	I Cor 7:1-24	31:19-24	21:4
12	Neh 3:15-5:13	I Cor 7:25-40	32:1-11	21:5-7
13	Neh 5:14-7:60	I Cor 8:1-13	33:1-12	21:8-10
14	Neh 7:61-9:21	I Cor 9:1-18	33:13-22	21:11-12
15	Neh 9:22-10:39	I Cor 9:19-10:13	34:1-10	21:13
16	Neh 11:1-12:26	I Cor 10:14-11:1	34:11-22	21:14-16
17	Neh 12:27-13:31	I Cor 11:2-16	35:1-16	21:17-18
18	Esther 1:1-3:15	I Cor 11:17-34	35:17-28	21:19-20
19	Esther 4:1-7:10	I Cor 12:1-26	36:1-12	21:21-22
20	Esther 8:1-10:3	I Cor 12:27-13:13	37:1-11	21:23-24
21	Job 1:1-3:26	I Cor 14:1-17	37:12-24	21:25-26
22	Job 4:1-7:21	I Cor 14:18-40	37:25-40	21:27
23	Job 8:1-11:20	I Cor 15:1-28	38:1-22	21:28-29
24	Job 12:1-15:35	I Cor 15:29-58	39:1-13	21:30-31
25	Job 16:1-19:29	I Cor 16:1-24	40:1-10	22:01
26	Job 20:1-22:30	II Cor 1:1-11	40:11-17	22:2-4
27	Job 23:1-27:23	II Cor 1:12-22	41:1-13	22:5-6
28	Job 28:1-30:31	II Cor 1:23-2:17	42:1-11	22:7
29	Job 31:1-33:33	II Cor 3:1-18	43:1-5	22:8-9
30	Job 34:1-36:33	II Cor 4:1-15	44:1-8	22:10-12
31	Job 37:1-39:30	II Cor 4:16-5:11	44:9-26	22:13

KEY PASSAGES:

_____
_____
_____
_____
_____
_____
_____
_____
_____
_____

PRAYER REQUESTS:

Date:	Request:	Date Answered:

AUGUST 2018

Sunday	Monday	Tuesday	Wednesday
			1
5	6	7	8
12	13	14	15
19	20	21	22
26	27	28	29

Thursday	Friday	Saturday	Notes
2	3	4	
9	10	11	
16	17	18	
23	24	25	
30	31		

SEPTEMBER 2018

	Old Testament	New Testament	Psalms	Proverbs
1	Job 40:1-42:17	II Cor 5:12-21	45:1-17	22:14
2	Eccl 1:1-3:22	II Cor 6:1-10	46:1-11	22:15
3	Eccl 4:1-6:12	II Cor 6:11-7:7	47:1-9	22:16
4	Eccl 7:1-9:18	II Cor 7:8-16	48:1-14	22:17-19
5	Eccl 10:1-12:14	II Cor 8:1-15	49:1-20	22:20-21
6	Song 1:1-4:16	II Cor 8:16-24	50:1-23	22:22-23
7	Song 5:1-8:14	II Cor 9:1-15	51:1-19	22:24-25
8	Isaiah 1:1-2:22	II Cor 10:1-18	52:1-9	22:26-27
9	Isaiah 3:1-5:30	II Cor 11:1-15	53:1-6	22:28-29
10	Isaiah 6:1-7:25	II Cor 11:16-33	54:1-7	23:1-3
11	Isaiah 8:1-9:21	II Cor 12:1-10	55:1-23	23:4-5
12	Isaiah 10:1-11:16	II Cor 12:11-21	56:1-13	23:6-8
13	Isaiah 12:1-14:32	II Cor 13:1-14	57:1-11	23:9-11
14	Isaiah 15:1-18:7	Gal 1:1-24	58:1-11	23:12
15	Isaiah 19:1-21:17	Gal 2:1-16	59:1-17	23:13-14
16	Isaiah 22:1-24:23	Gal 2:17-3:9	60:1-12	23:15-16
17	Isaiah 25:1-28:15	Gal 3:10-25	61:1-8	23:17-18
18	Isaiah 28:16-30:11	Gal 3:26-4:31	62:1-12	23:19-21
19	Isaiah 30:12-33:9	Gal 5:1-15	63:1-11	23:22
20	Isaiah 33:10-36:22	Gal 5:16-26	64:1-10	23:23
21	Isaiah 37:1-38:22	Gal 6:1-18	65:1-13	23:24
22	Isaiah 39:1-41:20	Eph 1:1-23	66:1-20	23:25-28
23	Isaiah 41:21-43:21	Eph 2:1-22	67:1-7	23:29-35
24	Isaiah 43:22-45:13	Eph 3:1-21	68:1-18	24:1-2
25	Isaiah 45:14-48:11	Eph 4:1-16	68:19-35	24:3-4
26	Isaiah 48:12-50:11	Eph 4:17-32	69:1-18	24:5-6
27	Isaiah 51:1-53:12	Eph 5:1-33	69:19-36	24:7
28	Isaiah 54:1-57:13	Eph 6:1-24	70:1-5	24:8
29	Isaiah 57:14-59:21	Phil 1:1-26	71:1-24	24:9-10
30	Isaiah 60:1-62:5	Phil 1:27-2:18	72:1-20	24:11-12

KEY PASSAGES:

_____
_____
_____
_____
_____
_____
_____
_____
_____
_____

PRAYER REQUESTS:

Date:	Request:	Date Answered:

SEPTEMBER 2018

Sunday	Monday	Tuesday	Wednesday
2	3 Labor Day	4	5
9	10	11 Patriot Day	12
16	17	18	19
23 30	24	25	26

Thursday	Friday	Saturday	Notes
		1	
6	7	8	
13	14	15	
20	21	22	
27	28	29	

OCTOBER 2018

	Old Testament	New Testament	Psalms	Proverbs
1	Isaiah 62:6-64:12	Phil 2:19-3:6	73:1-28	24:13-14
2	Isaiah 65:1-66:24	Phil 3:7-4:1	74:1-23	24:15-16
3	Jer 1:1-2:30	Phil 4:2-23	75:1-10	24:17-20
4	Jer 2:31-4:18	Col 1:1-23	76:1-12	24:21-22
5	Jer 4:19-6:15	Col 1:24-2:10	77:1-20	24:23-25
6	Jer 6:16-8:7	Col 2:11-23	78:1-31	24:26
7	Jer 8:8-9:26	Col 3:1-17	78:32-55	24:27
8	Jer 10:1-11:23	Col 3:18-4:18	78:56-72	24:28-29
9	Jer 12:1-14:10	I Thes 1:1-2:12	79:1-13	24:30-34
10	Jer 14:11-16:13	I Thes 2:13-3:13	80:1-19	25:1-5
11	Jer 16:14-18:23	I Thes 4:1-5:3	81:1-16	25:6-7
12	Jer 19:1-21:14	I Thes 5:4-28	82:1-8	25:8-10
13	Jer 22:1-23:20	II Thes 1:1-12	83:1-18	25:11-13
14	Jer 23:21-25:38	II Thes 2:1-17	84:1-12	25:14-15
15	Jer 26:1-27:22	II Thes 3:1-18	85:1-13	25:16
16	Jer 28:1-29:32	I Tim 1:1-20	86:1-17	25:17
17	Jer 30:1-31:22	I Tim 2:1-15	87:1-7	25:18-19
18	Jer 31:23-32:44	I Tim 3:1-16	88:1-18	25:20-22
19	Jer 33:1-34:22	I Tim 4:1-16	89:1-18	25:23-24
20	Jer 35:1-36:32	I Tim 5:1-25	89:19-37	25:25-27
21	Jer 37:1-38:28	I Tim 6:1-21	89:38-52	25:28
22	Jer 39:1-41:18	II Tim 1:1-18	90:1-91:16	26:1-2
23	Jer 42:1-44:23	II Tim 2:1-21	92:1-93:5	26:3-5
24	Jer 44:24-47:7	II Tim 2:22-3:17	94:1-23	26:6-8
25	Jer 48:1-49:22	II Tim 4:1-22	95:1-96:13	26:9-12
26	Jer 49:23-50:46	Titus 1:1-16	97:1-98:9	26:13-16
27	Jer 51:1-53	Titus 2:1-15	99:1-9	26:17
28	Jer 51:54-52:34	Titus 3:1-15	100:1-5	26:18-19
29	Lam 1:1-2:22	Phile 1-25	101:1-8	26:20
30	Lam 3:1-66	Heb 1:1-14	102:1-28	26:21-22
31	Lam 4-5:22	Heb. 2:1-18	103:1-22	26:23

KEY PASSAGES:

_____
_____
_____
_____
_____
_____
_____
_____
_____
_____

PRAYER REQUESTS:

Date:	Request:	Date Answered:

OCTOBER 2018

Sunday	Monday	Tuesday	Wednesday
	1	2	3
7	8 Columbus Day	9	10
14	15	16	17
21	22	23	24
28	29	30	31

Thursday	Friday	Saturday	Notes
4	5	6	
11	12	13	
18	19	20	
25	26	27	

NOVEMBER 2018

	Old Testament	New Testament	Psalms	Proverbs
1	Eze 1:1-3:15	Heb 3:1-19	104:1-18	26:24-26
2	Eze 3:16-6:14	Heb 4:1-16	104:19-35	26:27
3	Eze 7:1-9:11	Heb 5:1-14	105:1-15	26:28
4	Eze 10:1-11:25	Heb 6:1-20	105:16-36	27:1-2
5	Eze 12:1-14:11	Heb 7:1-17	105:37-45	27:3
6	Eze 14:12-16:43	Heb 7:18-28	106:1-23	27:4-6
7	Eze 16:44-17:24	Heb 8:1-13	106:24-48	27:7-9
8	Eze 18:1-19:14	Heb 9:1-15	107:1-16	27:10
9	Eze 20:1-49	Heb 9:16-28	107:17-43	27:11
10	Eze 21:1-22:31	Heb 10:1-18	108:1-13	27:12
11	Eze 23:1-49	Heb 10:19-39	109:1-31	27:13
12	Eze 24:1-26:21	Heb 11:1-16	110:1-7	27:14
13	Eze 27:1-28:26	Heb 11:17-29	111:1-10	27:15-16
14	Eze 29:1-30:26	Heb 11:30-12:11	112:1-10	27:17
15	Eze 31:1-32:32	Heb 12:12-29	113:1-114:8	27:18-20
16	Eze 33:1-34:31	Heb 13:1-25	115:1-18	27:21-22
17	Eze 35:1-36:38	James 1:1-18	116:1-19	27:23-27
18	Eze 37:1-38:23	James 1:19-2:13	117:1-2	28:1
19	Eze 39:1-40:27	James 2:14-3:18	118:1-18	28:2
20	Eze 40:28-41:26	James 4:1-17	118:19-29	28:3-5
21	Eze 42:1-43:27	James 5:1-20	119:1-16	28:6-7
22	Eze 44:1-45:9	I Pet 1:1-12	119:17-32	28:8-10
23	Eze 45:10-46:24	I Pet 1:13-2:10	119:33-48	28:11
24	Eze 47:1-48:35	I Pet 2:11-3:7	119:49-64	28:12-13
25	Dan 1:1-2:23	I Pet 3:8-4:6	119:65-80	28:14
26	Dan 2:24-3:30	I Pet 4:7-5:14	119:81-96	28:15-16
27	Dan 4:1-37	II Pet 1:1-21	119:97-112	28:17-18
28	Dan 5:1-31	II Pet 2:1-22	119:113-128	28:19-20
29	Dan 6:1-28	II Pet 3:1-18	119:129-152	28:21-22
30	Dan 7:1-28	I John 1:1-10	119:153-176	28:23-24

KEY PASSAGES:

_____
_____
_____
_____
_____
_____
_____
_____
_____
_____

PRAYER REQUESTS:

Date:	Request:	Date Answered:

NOVEMBER 2018

Sunday	Monday	Tuesday	Wednesday
4 Daylight Saving (End)	5	6	7
11 Veteran's Day	12	13	14
18	19	20	21
25	26	27	28

Thursday	Friday	Saturday	Notes
1	2	3	
8	9	10	
15	16	17	
22 Thanksgiving	23	24	
29	30		

DECEMBER 2018

	Old Testament	New Testament	Psalms	Proverbs
1	Dan 8:1-27	I John 2:1-17	120:1-7	28:25-26
2	Dan 9:1-11:1	I John 2:18-3:9	121:1-8	28:27-28
3	Dan 11:2-45	I John 3:10-24	122:1-9	29:1
4	Dan 12:1-13	I John 4:1-21	123:1-4	29:2-4
5	Hosea 1:1-3:5	I John 5:1-21	124:1-8	29:5-8
6	Hosea 4:1-5:15	II John 1-13	125:1-5	29:9-11
7	Hosea 6:1-9:17	III John 1-14	126:1-6	29:12-14
8	Hosea 10:1-14:9	Jude 1-25	127:1-5	29:15-17
9	Joel 1:1-3:21	Rev 1:1-20	128:1-6	29:18
10	Amos 1:1-3:15	Rev 2:1-17	129:1-8	29:19-20
11	Amos 4:1-6:14	Rev 2:18-3:6	130:1-8	29:21-22
12	Amos 7:1-9:15	Rev 3:7-22	131:1-3	29:23
13	Obadiah 1-21	Rev 4:1-11	132:1-18	29:24-25
14	Jonah 1:1-4:11	Rev. 5:1-14	133:1-3	29:26-27
15	Micah 1:1-4:13	Rev 6:1-17	134:1-3	30:1-4
16	Micah 5:1-7:20	Rev 7:1-17	135:1-21	30:5-6
17	Nahum 1:1-3:19	Rev 8:1-13	136:1-26	30:7-9
18	Habakkuk 1:1-3:19	Rev 9:1-21	137:1-9	30:10
19	Zeph. 1:1-3:20	Rev 10:1-11	138:1-8	30:11-14
20	Haggai 1:1-2:23	Rev 11:1-19	139:1-24	30:15-16
21	Zech 1:1-21	Rev 12:1-17	140:1-13	30:17
22	Zech 2:1-3:10	Rev 13:1-18	141:1-10	30:18-20
23	Zech 4:1-5:11	Rev 14:1-20	142:1-7	30:21-23
24	Zech 6:1-7:14	Rev 15:1-8	143:1-12	30:24-28
25	Zech 8:1-23	Rev 16:1-21	144:1-15	30:29-31
26	Zech 9:1-17	Rev 17:1-18	145:1-21	30:32
27	Zech 10:1-11:17	Rev 18:1-24	146:1-10	30:33
28	Zech 12:1-13:9	Rev 19:1-21	147:1-20	31:1-7
29	Zech 14:1-21	Rev 20:1-15	148:1-14	31:8-9
30	Malachi 1:1-2:17	Rev 21:1-27	149:1-9	31:10-24
31	Malachi 3:1-4:6	Rev 22:1-21	150:1-6	31:25-31

KEY PASSAGES:

PRAYER REQUESTS:

Date: **Request:**   **Date Answered:**

DECEMBER 2018

Sunday	Monday	Tuesday	Wednesday
2	3	4	5
9	10	11	12
16	17	18	19
23	24	25	26
30	31 New Year's Eve	Christmas Day	

Thursday	Friday	Saturday	Notes
		1	
6	7	8	
13	14	15	
20	21	22	
27	28	29	

Date:

Date:

Date:

Date:

Date:

Date:

Date:

Date:

Date: _____

Date:

Date:

Date:

Date:

Date:

Date:

Date:

Date:

Date:

Date:

Date:

Date:

Date:

Date:

Date:

Date:

Date:

Date:

Date:

Date:

Date: _____

Date:

Date: _____

Date:

Date:

Date:

Date: _____

Date:

Date:

Date:

Date: _____

Date:

Date:

Date:

Date:

Date:

Date: _____

Date:

Date: _____

Date:

Date:

Date: _____

Date:

Date:

Date:

Date:

Date:

Date:

Date:

Date:

Date:

Date:

Date:

Date:

Date:

Date:

Date:

Date: _____
_____
_____
_____
_____
_____
_____
_____
_____
_____
_____
_____
_____
_____
_____
_____
_____
_____
_____
_____
_____
_____
_____
_____
_____
_____
_____
_____
_____
_____
_____
_____
_____

Date:

Date:

Date:

Date:

Date:

Date: _____

Date:

Date:

Date:

Date:

Date:

Date:

Date: _____

Date:

Date:

Date: _____

Date:

Date:

Date:

Date:

Date:

Date: _____

Date:

Date:

Date:

Date:

Date:

Date:

Date:

Date:

Date:

Date:

Date:

Date:

Date:

Date:

2019

January

Sun	Mon	Tue	Wed	Thu	Fri	Sat
30	31	1	2	3	4	5
6	7	8	9	10	11	12
13	14	15	16	17	18	19
20	21	22	23	24	25	26
27	28	29	30	31	1	2
3	4	5	6	7	8	9

February

Sun	Mon	Tue	Wed	Thu	Fri	Sat
27	28	29	30	31	1	2
3	4	5	6	7	8	9
10	11	12	13	14	15	16
17	18	19	20	21	22	23
24	25	26	27	28	1	2
3	4	5	6	7	8	9

March

Sun	Mon	Tue	Wed	Thu	Fri	Sat
24	25	26	27	28	1	2
3	4	5	6	7	8	9
10	11	12	13	14	15	16
17	18	19	20	21	22	23
24	25	26	27	28	29	30
31	1	2	3	4	5	6

April

Sun	Mon	Tue	Wed	Thu	Fri	Sat
31	1	2	3	4	5	6
7	8	9	10	11	12	13
14	15	16	17	18	19	20
21	22	23	24	25	26	27
28	29	30	1	2	3	4
5	6	7	8	9	10	11

May

Sun	Mon	Tue	Wed	Thu	Fri	Sat
28	29	30	1	2	3	4
5	6	7	8	9	10	11
12	13	14	15	16	17	18
19	20	21	22	23	24	25
26	27	28	29	30	31	1
2	3	4	5	6	7	8

June

Sun	Mon	Tue	Wed	Thu	Fri	Sat
26	27	28	29	30	31	1
2	3	4	5	6	7	8
9	10	11	12	13	14	15
16	17	18	19	20	21	22
23	24	25	26	27	28	29
30	1	2	3	4	5	6

July

Sun	Mon	Tue	Wed	Thu	Fri	Sat
30	1	2	3	4	5	6
7	8	9	10	11	12	13
14	15	16	17	18	19	20
21	22	23	24	25	26	27
28	29	30	31	1	2	3
4	5	6	7	8	9	10

August

Sun	Mon	Tue	Wed	Thu	Fri	Sat
28	29	30	31	1	2	3
4	5	6	7	8	9	10
11	12	13	14	15	16	17
18	19	20	21	22	23	24
25	26	27	28	29	30	31
1	2	3	4	5	6	7

September

Sun	Mon	Tue	Wed	Thu	Fri	Sat
1	2	3	4	5	6	7
8	9	10	11	12	13	14
15	16	17	18	19	20	21
22	23	24	25	26	27	28
29	30	1	2	3	4	5
6	7	8	9	10	11	12

October

Sun	Mon	Tue	Wed	Thu	Fri	Sat
29	30	1	2	3	4	5
6	7	8	9	10	11	12
13	14	15	16	17	18	19
20	21	22	23	24	25	26
27	28	29	30	31	1	2
3	4	5	6	7	8	9

November

Sun	Mon	Tue	Wed	Thu	Fri	Sat
27	28	29	30	31	1	2
3	4	5	6	7	8	9
10	11	12	13	14	15	16
17	18	19	20	21	22	23
24	25	26	27	28	29	30
1	2	3	4	5	6	7

December

Sun	Mon	Tue	Wed	Thu	Fri	Sat
1	2	3	4	5	6	7
8	9	10	11	12	13	14
15	16	17	18	19	20	21
22	23	24	25	26	27	28
29	30	31	1	2	3	4
5	6	7	8	9	10	11

Made in the USA
Lexington, KY
08 January 2018